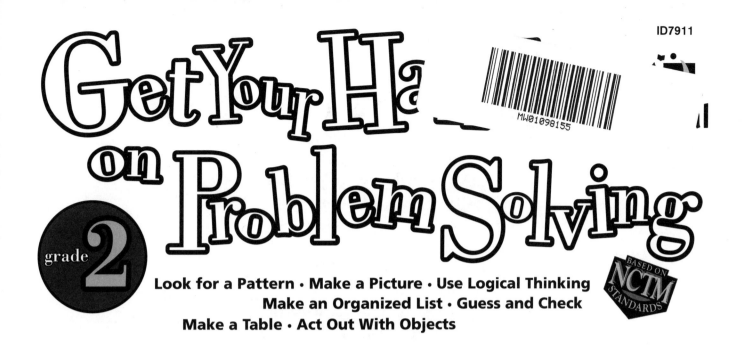

Get Your Hands on Problem Solving

on Problem Solving

grade 2

Look for a Pattern · Make a Picture · Use Logical Thinking
Make an Organized List · Guess and Check
Make a Table · Act Out With Objects

BASED ON NCTM STANDARDS

ID7911
MW01098155

CAT FOOD

by Judy Goodnow & Shirley Hoogeboom

Judy Goodnow and Shirley Hoogeboom are authors, curriculum developers, and editors for Ideal School Supply Company. Together they have taught children at the kindergarten level through grade six. As curriculum developers, they have each authored or coauthored over 100 books and sets of games and activities for reading, language arts, and math. They have conducted workshops for teachers in the use of math manipulatives and computer-related materials.

Judy holds a bachelor of arts degree from Wellesley College, a master's degree in Interactive Educational Technology from Stanford University, and earned her California Teaching Credential at San Jose State University.

Shirley holds a bachelor of arts degree in Education from Calvin College where she earned her Michigan Teaching Credential. She completed further studies in education at the University of Minnesota and earned her California Teaching Credential at California State University, Hayward.

Art Director: Nancy Tseng
Cover Design: Lee McCoy Creative Center
Illustrations: Duane Bibby
Text Design and Production: London Road Design, Redwood City, CA

ISBN: 1-56451-255-X
Get Your Hands on Problem Solving, Grade 2
© 1998 Ideal School Supply
A Division of Instructional Fair Group, Inc.
A Tribune Education Company
3195 Wilson Drive NW, Grand Rapids, MI 49544 • USA
Duke Street, Wisbech, Cambs, PE13 2AE • UK
All Rights Reserved • Printed in USA

Table of Contents

Notes to the Teacher   iv
Four-Step Plan for Problem Solving   vii
Problem-Solving Strategies   viii
Cross-Reference Chart   x
Assessment Ideas   xi
Children's Books as Resources for Creating Problems   xii
Blackline Master for Dinosaurs   xiii
Blackline Master for Play Coins   xiv
Solutions   xv

Teaching Plan for Story Problem 1: **Look for a Pattern, Act Out With Objects**   1
Teaching Plan for Story Problem 2: **Look for a Pattern, Act Out With Objects**   2
Story Problems 1–6   3

Teaching Plan for Story Problem 7: **Make a Picture**   9
Teaching Plan for Story Problem 8: **Make a Picture**   10
Story Problems 7–12   11

Teaching Plan for Story Problem 13: **Use Logical Thinking, Act Out
  With Objects**   17
Teaching Plan for Story Problem 14: **Use Logical Thinking**   18
Story Problems 13–18   19

Teaching Plan for Story Problem 19: **Guess and Check, Act Out With Objects**   25
Teaching Plan for Story Problem 20: **Guess and Check, Act Out With Objects**   26
Story Problems 19–24   27

Teaching Plan for Story Problem 25: **Make a Table, Act Out With Objects**   33
Teaching Plan for Story Problem 26: **Make a Table, Act Out With Objects**   34
Story Problems 25–30   35

Teaching Plan for Story Problem 31: **Make an Organized List, Act Out
  With Objects**   41
Teaching Plan for Story Problem 32: **Make an Organized List, Act Out
  With Objects**   42
Story Problems 31–36   43

Practice Story Problems 37–52   49

Notes to the Teacher

This is the second in a series of books designed to help students become confident problem solvers:

> Get Your Hands on Problem Solving, Grade 1
> **Get Your Hands on Problem Solving, Grade 2**
> Get Your Hands on Problem Solving, Grade 3

The activities in this series introduce students to nonroutine logic and math story problems, plus a four-step plan and seven strategies for solving them. One of the strategies—Act Out With Objects—is often used in combination with the other strategies: Look for a Pattern, Make a Picture, Use Logical Thinking, Guess and Check, Make a Table, and Make an Organized List.

These strategies are tools that students can use for solving a variety of problems. The activities in this book help children develop a sense of which strategies will be most useful for solving given problems. Learning to use the strategies helps children build confidence in their ability to solve problems.

The National Council of Teachers of Mathematics (NCTM) stresses that "Problem solving should be the central focus of the mathematics curriculum. . . . Ideally, students should share their thinking and approaches with other students and with teachers, and they should learn several ways of representing problems and strategies for solving them. In addition, they should learn to value the process of solving problems as much as they value the solutions. . . . A major goal of problem-solving instruction is to enable children to develop and apply strategies to solve problems."

Contents
This book presents logic and math story problems at a simple level. The stories often show humorous animal characters in situations that are familiar to children.

There are six sections of story problems that can be used to introduce the problem-solving process and strategies. Each section includes six story problem activity sheets, plus teaching plans for the first two story problems. The teaching plans give sample teacher-and-student dialogs that model the problem-solving process and the use of the strategy being introduced. Some also suggest that children act out the problem with objects.

Examples:

Teaching Plan   Story Problem Activity Sheet

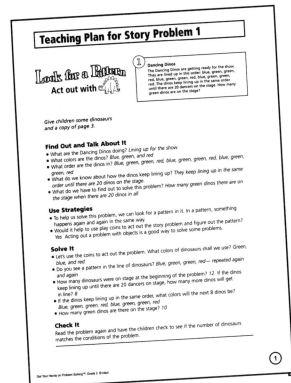

In each section, the first and second problems and teaching plans introduce the children to two different types of problems that they can solve with the same strategy. There are two more problems of each type within the section.

The story problem activity sheets name the strategy or strategies being introduced, and, when appropriate, show an icon of the objects children can use to act out the problem. They give one story problem, plus a Doing More or Your Turn activity for the children to do after they have solved the story problem. The Doing More activities are extensions of the problem, and the Your Turn activities encourage children to create their own problems for their peers to solve.

There are 16 practice story problems on pages 49–64, which can be used for assessment and/or for additional practice. Children will be able to choose the strategy or strategies they think will be most helpful for solving the problem.

The objects suggested for the story problems in this book are plastic or paper dinosaurs; plastic or paper play coins; and colored linking cubes or squares of paper. Linking Cubes (ID7617), Dinosaurs (ID7667), and Plastic Coins (ID7509) are available from Ideal or any Ideal dealer. Blackline masters for paper dinosaurs and coins are provided on pages xiii and xiv.

The Four-Step Plan and Problem-Solving Strategies that will be used for solving the story problems are explained on pages vii–ix.

In the Cross-Reference Chart on page x, a strategy is suggested for each problem. However, children should be encouraged to use whatever strategy they find most helpful, including ones that they devise themselves.

Assessment Ideas are given on page xi, and Solutions are provided on pages xv–xvi. If you wish to create more problems similar to those included in this book, the children's books listed on page xii may provide a rich resource for familiar characters and contexts.

Teaching Suggestions

It is recommended that children work together in pairs. This kind of grouping allows children to talk together about what they are thinking and how they are solving the problems.

Give each child a copy of the story problem activity sheet, and a supply of dinosaurs or linking cubes or play money if any are suggested. (The story problems often use dinosaurs and linking cubes in a variety of colors, so you may want to let the children color the paper cutouts prior to the activities.)

Begin by reading the story problem to the children. Some children may need to hear it several times to retain the information. Invite the children to say the problem in their own words.

Then guide the children through the problem-solving process, following the teaching plan or your own plan for that story problem. (In the teaching plans provided, the dialogs include sample questions you might ask, and, in italics, some possible answers children might give.) Begin by asking questions to help the children find all of the information in the problem that they will need to solve it. Next, talk about the strategies, or tools, that can be used to solve the problem. Help the children use the strategies, and encourage them to talk about their thinking as they solve the problem. At this stage, the development of math language and reasoning is more important than getting the right answer. The children may even discover their own unique ways of solving the problem that they will use again and again. They are building a library of ways to think about and solve problems, and at the same time are building confidence in themselves as problem solvers.

If you are working with young children, you may simply want to let them work out the problems with manipulatives, then talk about their answers. With older children, you may want to have them record their answers as suggested on the activity sheet.

After the children have solved a story problem, reread the story while they check to see that their solutions meet all the conditions given in the problem.

A Four-Step Plan for Problem Solving

Step one is to **FIND OUT AND TALK ABOUT IT.** In this beginning step, children find out what the problem means and what question must be answered to solve it. It is important that children know the meaning of all the words used in the story problem and understand what is going on in the problem. They should also learn how to find each piece of important information.

Step two is to choose and **USE STRATEGIES.** In this step, children begin to think about the tools they can use to solve the problem and which tools will be most helpful.

Step three is to **SOLVE IT.** In this step, children use the strategy and any objects suggested to find a solution to the problem. On many of the student activity pages, pictures or tables or organized lists have been started to introduce the strategy to the children. Help the children complete them and use them to solve the problem. The children can also record their solutions in the ways suggested on the student pages.

Step four is to **CHECK IT.** In this step, the children should review their work and solution while you reread the problem. They need to make sure their solution fits with the clues and information given in the problem.

Problem-Solving Strategies

Act Out With Objects • Children will use dinosuars, linking cubes, and play coins and bills to act out many of the story problems in this book. Being able to act out the story with these objects helps children visualize what is going on in the problem, understand the underlying math concepts, and work out the solution.

Look for a Pattern • A pattern is a regular, systematic repetition. Identifying the pattern helps the problem solver predict what will "come next." In story problems 1 through 6, children will identify and continue visual patterns and number patterns.

 Ice-Skating on Flora's Pond
Flora Frog is teaching dinos to ice-skate on her pond. There are 25 dinos. They are lined up in this order: yellow, yellow, blue, blue, green, yellow, yellow, blue, blue, green, and so on. How many blue dinos are there in the line?

Make a Picture • Making pictures or diagrams, such as number lines and maps, can be very useful for solving some problems. In story problems 7 through 12, children will be completing pictures of floors in a building (a type of number line) or other map-like drawings to solve the problems.

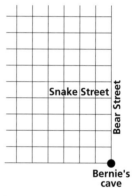

Use Logical Thinking • Logical reasoning is really used in all problem solving. Logical thinking is especially needed, however, for the types of problems that include or imply conditional statements such as "If . . . then," or "If . . . then . . . else." Story problems 13 through 18 give some clues, and the children will use "If . . . then" kind of thinking to fill in missing information and solve the problems.

 Dinos Out for a Ride
A yellow dino, a red dino, and two blue dinos are out for a ride in a car. The dino who is driving is not yellow or blue. A blue dino is sitting behind a yellow dino. What color is each dino in the car?

Guess and Check • In some story problems, information is given in an indirect way. Students have to make a guess for one number, or a sum of numbers, in order to work out the problem. Then they check to see if the solution is correct. If not, they use the information from the incorrect guess to make another more informed guess. Children use this strategy to solve story problems 19 through 24.

> 4 nickels, 8 pennies
> 5+5+5+1+1+1+1+1+1+1+1=28¢   too low
> 5 nickels, 10 pennies
> 5+5+5+5+5+1+1+1+1+1+1+1+1+1+1=35¢   yes

Make a Table • Problem solvers find that making tables helps them organize and keep track of information, discover missing information, and identify data that is asked for in the problem. The recording spaces for story problems 25 through 30 show the beginnings of tables. Problem solvers will find that tables can be made in many different forms, for example T-charts, vertical tables, and horizontal tables.

15 Cents

Dimes	Nickels	Pennies
1	1	0
1	0	5

Make an Organized List • Making an organized list helps problem solvers organize and keep track of their work with the data. This kind of step-by-step approach to solving the problem makes it easier for the problem solver to review what steps have been taken and pinpoint what steps still need to be completed. An organized approach is particularly helpful when a problem solver needs to find ALL of the possible solutions; for example, all the ways that a group of colored bears can be combined in pairs. The recording spaces for story problems 31 through 36 show the beginnings of organized lists.

Picture	Colors of Dinos
1	blue, blue
2	
3	

Cross-Reference Chart

Teaching Story Problems	Strategies and Manipulatives
1, 3, 4	Look for a Pattern, Act Out With Objects (dinosaurs)
2	Look for a Pattern, Act Out With Objects (coins)
5, 6	Look for a Pattern, Act Out With Objects (cubes)
7, 8, 9, 10, 11, 12	Make a Picture
13, 15, 17	Use Logical Thinking, Act Out With Objects (dinosaurs)
14, 16, 18	Use Logical Thinking
19, 21, 23	Guess and Check, Act Out With Objects (dinosaurs)
20, 22, 24	Guess and Check, Act Out With Objects (coins)
25, 27, 29	Make a Table, Act Out With Objects (coins)
26, 28	Make a Table, Act Out With Objects (dinosaurs)
30	Make a Table, Act Out With Objects (cubes)
31, 33, 35	Make an Organized List, Act Out With Objects (dinosaurs)
32, 34, 36	Make an Organized List, Act Out With Objects (coins)

Practice Story Problems	Strategies and Manipulatives*
37	Guess and Check, Act Out With Objects (coins)
38	Look for a Pattern, Act Out With Objects (cubes)
39	Make a Table, Act Out With Objects (coins)
40	Use Logical Thinking
41	Make a Picture
42	Guess and Check, Act Out With Objects (coins)
43	Make an Organized List, Act Out With Objects (cubes)
44	Look for a Pattern, Act Out With Objects (dinosaurs)
45	Use Logical Thinking, Act Out With Objects (dinosaurs)
46	Make an Organized List, Act Out With Objects (dinosaurs)
47	Make a Picture
48	Make a Table, Act Out With Objects (dinosaurs)
49	Look for a Pattern, Act Out With Objects (cubes)
50	Make an Organized List, Act Out With Objects (coins)
51	Make a Table, Act Out With Objects (cubes)
52	Guess and Check, Act Out With Objects (dinosaurs)

* The strategies and manipulatives shown can be used for solving the practice problems; however, children may choose to use other strategies and solve the problems without the use of manipulatives.

Assessment Ideas

These problems provide an excellent opportunity for assessing your students' reasoning skills and mathematical understanding. You can use any of the problems as an informal assessment tool or in combination with the simple scoring rubric shown below. You may prefer to use a scoring rubric that is part of your school district's curriculum, if that is available. Different numbers of levels are possible in a scoring rubric; we have shown only three.

With these problem-solving activities, it is more important to evaluate the students' reasoning skills and mathematical thinking than to concentrate on arithmetic or computation skills. Allow for computational errors, if a student shows an understanding of how to use a problem-solving strategy and has provided sound reasoning for how to solve the problem.

For informal assessment, you can record observations of the students as they work together to solve a problem. As you make your observations, you will want to concentrate on how the students communicate with one another: Do they contribute ideas, question ideas, show initiative, explain their thinking? Also note how they work with a partner or group: Do they build on ideas, exchange ideas, listen to ideas, work cooperatively? Also observe how they use the manipulatives: Do they use them in appropriate ways, revealing an understanding of the problem?

Here is a simple scoring rubric that you can use:

Needs Improvement
Does not understand the problem question
Cannot extract relevant information from the problem
Does not communicate clear thinking
Makes major errors

Good
Seems to understand the problem question
Extracts some relevant information from the problem
Shows an attempt to work out the problem
Communicates thinking, but not adequate mathematical reasoning

Very Good
Understands the problem question
Extracts relevant information from the problem
Communicates thinking clearly
Demonstrates mathematical thinking
Provides a complete solution which shows understanding of the
  problem-solving process

Children's Books as Resources for Creating Problems

Children's literature offers a wealth of characters and settings for creating story problems similar to the ones in this book. Imagine the delight of children when they discover their favorite storybook characters in the problems! This gives the children greater incentive for solving the problems, and helps them connect mathematics with literature. They may even use your story problems as models for creating their own storybook problems.

The following children's books are just a few of the many that can be used as resources for problems. Most of them can be used for more than one strategy. You can also use favorite characters from the books your children are reading and from familiar folktales.

Look for a Pattern
The Doorbell Rang, by Pat Hutchins
Mrs. Gaddy and the Fast-Growing Vine,
by Wilson Gage
Mouse Tales, by Arnold Lobel

Make a Picture
The Fire Cat, by Esther Averill
Frog and Toad Together, by Arnold Lobel
Henry and Mudge, by Cynthia Rylant

Guess and Check
The Tree Stump, by Chris Forbes
Arthur's Honey Bear, by Lillian Hoban
*Alexander Who Used to Be Rich Last
Sunday,* by Judith Viorst

Make a Table
How Many Feet in the Bed?
by Diane J. Hamm
Across the Stream, by Mirra Ginsburg

Use Logical Thinking
D.W. the Picky Eater, by Marc Brown
Which Witch Is Which, by Pat Hutchins
Hats, Hats, Hats, by Ann Morris
Frog and Toad Are Friends, by Arnold Lobel

Make an Organized List
Ten What? A Mystery Counting Book,
by Russell Hoban
King Henry's Palace, by Pat Hutchins
A Three Hat Day, by Laura Geringer
Arthur's Funny Money, by Lillian Hoban
Henry and Mudge and the Forever Sea,
by Cynthia Rylant

Here is one example of a story problem using a character and setting from *Arthur's Funny Money:*

Arthur's Bike Wash

Arthur scrubbed and shined Peter's bike. Then he washed Peter's fire engine, sled, and wagon. Peter took 8 coins out of his pocket to pay Arthur. Violet wrote down 36 cents. What coins did Peter take out of his pocket?

Dinosaurs

Play Coins

Solutions

Story Problem

1	10
2	30¢
3	10
4	2
5	8 blue, 8 green, 4 purple, 4 pink
6	18
7	9 floors

8

9	12 floors

10
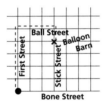

11	11 floors

12
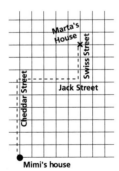

13
red	yellow
blue	blue

14 Riding on Trains

15
red	green
yellow	blue
or
green	red
blue	yellow

16 bumblebee

17
blue	yellow	red
yellow	blue	red

18 soccer

19 1 red, 2 yellow, 3 green

20 5 nickels, 10 pennies
Doing More:
2 dimes, 2 nickels, 5 pennies

21 1 blue, 2 red, 3 yellow

22 3 dimes, 6 nickels, 3 pennies
Doing More:
13 pennies, 4 nickels, 3 dimes

23 1 green, 2 red, 3 blue, 4 yellow

24 4 nickels, 4 dimes, 1 quarter
Doing More:
4 dimes, 8 nickels, 5 pennies

25 28¢

26 20

27 24¢; Doing More: 31¢

28 15

29 36¢ or 40¢

30 48

31 blue, blue
blue, yellow
yellow, yellow

32
Dimes	Nickels	Pennies
1	1	0
1	0	5
0	3	0
0	2	5
0	1	10
0	0	15

33   red, red
red, yellow
red, blue
yellow, yellow
yellow, blue
blue, blue

34

Dimes	Nickels	Pennies
2	0	0
1	2	0
1	1	5
1	0	10
0	4	0
0	3	5
0	2	10
0	1	15
0	0	20

35   green, green
green, blue
blue, blue
yellow, yellow
yellow, red
red, red

36

Dimes	Nickels	Pennies
2	0	1
1	2	1
1	1	6
1	0	11
0	4	1
0	3	6
0	2	11
0	1	16
0	0	21

37   3 dimes, 2 nickels, 1 quarter

38   12 yellow, 6 brown, 6 orange

39   53¢ or 57¢

40   train

41   8 birdhouses

42   2 quarters, 2 dimes, 4 nickels, 8 pennies

43   green, green
green, purple
green, orange
purple, purple
purple, orange
orange, orange

44   13

45

blue	red	blue
green	green	yellow

or

blue	red	blue
yellow	green	green

46   green, green, blue
green, blue, blue
green, yellow, yellow
blue, yellow, yellow
or
green, green, green
blue, blue, blue
yellow, yellow, yellow,
green, blue, yellow
Other solutions are possible.

47

48   56

49   19

50

Dimes	Nickels	Pennies
2	1	0
2	0	5
1	3	0
1	2	5
1	1	10
1	0	15
0	5	0
0	4	5
0	3	10
0	2	15
0	1	20
0	0	25

51   25

52   1 blue, 2 red, 3 yellow, 4 green

Teaching Plan for Story Problem 1

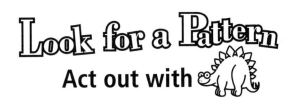

Act out with

> **① Dancing Dinos**
> The Dancing Dinos are getting ready for the show. They are lined up in this order: blue, green, green, red, blue, green, green, red, blue, green, green, red. The dinos keep lining up in the same order until there are 20 dancers on the stage. How many green dinos are on the stage?

Give children some dinosaurs and a copy of page 3.

Find Out and Talk About It

- What are the Dancing Dinos doing? *Lining up for the show*
- What colors are the dinos? *Blue, green, and red*
- What order are the dinos in? *Blue, green, green, red, blue, green, green, red, blue, green, green, red*
- What do we know about how the dinos keep lining up? *They keep lining up in the same order until there are 20 dinos on the stage.*
- What do we have to find out to solve this problem? *How many green dinos there are on the stage when there are 20 dinos in all*

Use Strategies

- To help us solve this problem, we can look for a pattern in it. In a pattern, something happens again and again in the same way.
- Would it help to use play dinos to act out the story problem and figure out the pattern? *Yes* Acting out a problem with objects is a good way to solve some problems.

Solve It

- Let's use the dinos to act out the problem. What colors of dinosaurs shall we use? *Green, blue, and red*
- Do you see a pattern in the line of dinosaurs? *Blue, green, green, red— repeated again and again*
- How many dinosaurs were on stage at the beginning of the problem? *12* If the dinos keep lining up until there are 20 dancers on stage, how many more dinos will get in line? *8*
- If the dinos keep lining up in the same order, what colors will the next 8 dinos be? *Blue, green, green, red, blue, green, green, red*
- How many green dinos are there on the stage? *10*

Check It

Read the problem again and have the children check to see if the number of dinosaurs matches the conditions of the problem.

Teaching Plan for Story Problem 2

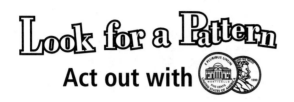

Act out with

> **② Albert and the Tooth Fairy**
> Albert Alligator's first tooth came out. Albert put his tooth under his pillow. The next morning he found 5 cents from the Tooth Fairy. When he lost his second tooth, Albert found 10 cents. When his third tooth came out, Albert found 15 cents. If the Tooth Fairy kept using the same pattern, how much money did Albert find when his sixth tooth came out?

Give children some play coins and a copy of page 4.

Find Out and Talk About It

- What was happening to Albert Alligator? *He was losing his teeth and finding money from the Tooth Fairy.*
- How much money did Albert find when his first tooth came out? *5 cents* When his second tooth came out? *10 cents* When his third tooth came out? *15 cents*
- What do we know about the way the Tooth Fairy was giving money to Albert? *The Tooth Fairy was using a pattern and giving Albert money each time a tooth came out.*
- What do we have to find out to solve this problem? *How much money Albert found when his sixth tooth came out*

Use Strategies

- To help us solve this problem, we can look for a pattern—something that happens again and again in the same way.
- Would it help to use play coins to figure out the pattern? *Yes* Acting out problems with objects is a good way to solve some problems.

Solve It

- How much money shall we take for Albert's first tooth? *5 cents* How much for his second tooth? *10 cents* How much for his third tooth? *15 cents*
- Do you see a pattern in the way the Tooth Fairy gives money to Albert? *For each tooth, she gives five cents more than for the tooth before it.* (Children may describe the pattern in other ways.)
- If the Tooth Fairy kept using that pattern, how much money did she give Albert when his fourth tooth came out? *20 cents* When his fifth tooth came out? *25 cents* How much money when his sixth tooth came out? *30 cents*

Check It

Read the problem again and have the children check to see if the money matches the conditions of the problem.

Name _____

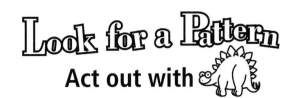
1 Dancing Dinos

The Dancing Dinos are getting ready for the show. They are lined up in this order: blue, green, green, red, blue, green, green, red, blue, green, green, red. The dinos keep lining up in the same order until there are 20 dancers on the stage. How many green dinos are on the stage?

Write the number. _____

Your Turn

If there are 30 dinosaurs in the line, how many blue dinosaurs will there be on the stage?

Name _____

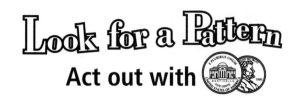

Act out with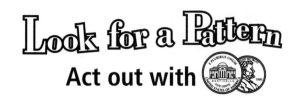

Albert and the Tooth Fairy

Albert Alligator's first tooth came out. Albert put his tooth under his pillow. The next morning he found 5 cents from the Tooth Fairy. When he lost his second tooth, Albert found 10 cents. When his third tooth came out, Albert found 15 cents. If the Tooth Fairy kept using the same pattern, how much money did Albert find when his sixth tooth came out?

Write the number. _____

Doing More

How much money will Albert find when his tenth tooth comes out? Tell a friend how you know.

(4)

Name _____

③ Ice-Skating on Flora's Pond

Flora Frog is teaching dinos to ice-skate on her pond. There are 25 dinos. They are lined up in this order: yellow, yellow, blue, blue, green, yellow, yellow, blue, blue, green, and so on. How many blue dinos are there in the line?

Write the number. _____

Your Turn

Make up your own pattern problem about the skating dinos. Let a friend solve your problem.

Name _____

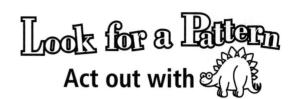

Peter Possum's Play

The dinos are coming to try out for Peter Possum's new play, "Beware of the Monstersaurus!" In the first hour, 12 dinos try out. In the second hour, 10 dinos try out. In the third hour, 8 dinos try out. In the fourth hour, 6 dinos try out. If the pattern continues, how many dinos will try out in the sixth hour? What a BIG Monstersaurus!

Write the number. _____

Doing More

If the pattern continues, how many dinos will try out in the seventh hour?

Name _____

5 Benny Delivers Mail

Benny the Mailbird is delivering mail to the mice on Mouse Lane. There are 24 mailboxes, and they are lined up in this order: blue, green, purple, blue, green, pink, blue, green, purple, blue, green, pink, and so on. How many mailboxes are there of each color?

Write the numbers.

blue _____   purple _____

green _____   pink _____

Your Turn

Make up your own pattern problem about mailboxes. Let a friend solve your problem.

Name _____

⑥ Catfish Soup!

Carla Cat sold catfish soup in her cafe this week. Cats came from everywhere to buy it! On Monday, Carla sold 3 bowls. On Tuesday, she sold 6 bowls. On Wednesday, she sold 9 bowls. On Thursday, she sold 12 bowls. If the pattern continued, how many bowls of catfish soup did Carla sell on Saturday?

Write the number. _____

Doing More

How many bowls of catfish soup did Carla sell in all this week? Make up a price for the soup. Find out how much money Carla made.

Teaching Plan for Story Problem 7

Make a Picture

The Mouse House Apartments
Matt Mouse lives on the third floor of Mouse House Apartments. Today he is visiting friends. First he goes up 4 floors to see Mindy. Then he goes down 2 floors to visit Manuel. Next he goes up 4 floors to see Mimi. She lives on the top floor. How many floors does Mouse House Apartments have?

Give children a copy of page 11.

Find Out and Talk About It
- What is Matt Mouse doing? *Visiting friends in his apartment house*
- What floor does Matt live on? *The third*
- Where does he go first from his apartment? *Up 4 floors to see Mindy*
- Where does he go next? *Down 2 floors to see Manuel*
- Where does he go now? *Up 4 floors to see Mimi*
- Where does Mimi live? *On the top floor*
- What do we have to find out to solve this problem? *How many floors the apartment house has*

Use Strategies
- Would it help to make a picture showing the floors? *Yes* For problems like this, we can often make a picture to help us "see" what is happening in the problem.

Solve It
- What do we know about the apartment house that we can show in the picture? *We know that Matt lives on the third floor*
- Where does he start from when he goes to visit? *The third floor*
- Where does he go first? *Up 4 floors* How many floors can we add above Matt's floor? *4*
- Where does he go next? *Down 2 floors*
- Where does he go now? *Up 4 floors* Do we need to draw more floors? *Yes, 2 more*
- Where is he now? *On the ninth floor*
- How many floors are in the building? *9*

Check It
Read the problem again and have the children check to see if their answer matches the conditions in the problem.

Where is Duck's Café?
Bernie Bear is giving Flora Frog directions to Duck's Café. He says, "Start at my cave. Go 4 blocks up Bear Street to Snake Street. Turn left on Snake Street and go forward 3 blocks to Duck Street. Then turn right on Duck Street and go forward 5 blocks. Now you will be at Duck's Café." Can you show Flora's path to Duck's Café?

Give children a copy of page 12.

Find Out and Talk About It

- What is Bernie Bear doing? *Giving directions to Flora Frog*
- Where is Flora going? *To Duck's Café*
- What is Bernie's first direction? *Start at my cave. Go 4 blocks up Bear Street to Snake Street.*
- What is Bernie's next direction? *Go left on Snake Street and go forward 3 blocks to Duck Street.*
- What is Bernie's last direction? *Turn right on Duck Street and go forward 5 blocks.*
- What do we have to find out to solve this problem? *How to show the path from Bernie's cave to Duck's Café*

Use Strategies

- Would it help to make a map to show all the different directions that Flora has to follow? *Yes* For problems like this, we can often make a picture or map to help us "see" what is happening in the problem.

Solve It

- A map has been started for us. We can add the names of the streets and draw Flora's path on it.
- Where does the path begin? *At Bernie's cave*
- How many blocks does Flora need to go on Bear Street? *4* What street will she come to? *Snake Street* Let's write Snake Street along that street.
- Then what direction does Flora go? *Left on Snake Street* How many blocks forward on Snake Street? *3* What street does she come to? *Duck Street*
- What direction does she go? *Right on Duck Street* How many blocks forward on Duck Street? *5* Where is she now? *At Duck's Café*

Check It

Read the problem again and have the children check to see if their path matches the conditions in the problem.

Name _____

The Mouse House Apartments

Matt Mouse lives on the third floor of Mouse House Apartments. Today he is visiting friends. First he goes up 4 floors to see Mindy. Then he goes down 2 floors to visit Manuel. Next he goes up 4 floors to see Mimi. She lives on the top floor. How many floors does Mouse House Apartments have?

Finish the picture of the floors.

| 3 |
| 2 |
| 1 |

Write the number. _____

Your Turn

Make up your own story about Matt and his friends at the Mouse House Apartments. See if a friend can show how many floors are in your apartment house.

Name _____

Where is Duck's Café?

Bernie Bear is giving Flora Frog directions to Duck's Café. He says, "Start at my cave. Go 4 blocks up Bear Street to Snake Street. Turn left on Snake Street and go forward 3 blocks to Duck Street. Then turn right on Duck Street and go forward 5 blocks. Now you will be at Duck's Café." Can you show Flora's path to Duck's Café?

Finish the map.
Show Flora's path.

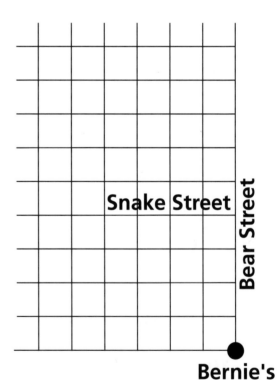

Doing More

Write directions for another path to Duck's Café.
Have a friend follow your directions.

Make a Picture

The Get-Well Building

Katie Kangaroo picks up mail from offices in the Get-Well Building. Katie is on the first floor. She goes up 5 floors and picks up mail from Dr. Mouse. Then she goes down 1 floor and gets mail from Dr. Possum. Next she goes up 7 floors to get mail from Dr. Cat on the top floor. How many floors are there in the Get-Well Building?

Finish the picture.

3
2
1

Write the number. _____

Your Turn

Make up your own story about Katie Kangaroo picking up mail from doctors' offices. See if a friend can solve your problem.

The Balloon Barn

Dolly Dog has directions to the Balloon Barn. The note says: "Begin at the corner of First Street and Bone Street. Go 5 blocks forward on First Street to Ball Street. Turn right on Ball Street and go forward 3 blocks to Stick Street. Turn right on Stick Street and go 1 block to the Balloon Barn. Can you show Dolly's path to the Balloon Barn?

Finish the map.
Show Dolly's path.

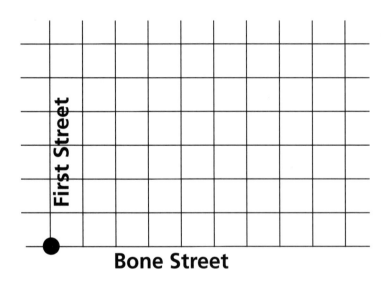

First Street

Bone Street

Doing More

Write directions for another way to the Balloon Barn.
Have a friend follow your directions.

Name _____

Make a Picture

11 Possum Hall

Polly Possum has just finished making jam. She is going to take some jars to her friends. Polly lives on the second floor in Possum Hall. She goes up 5 floors to give a jar to Penny. Then she goes down 3 floors to give a jar to Peter. Then she goes up 7 floors to give a jar to Paula. Paula lives on the top floor. How many floors are there in Possum Hall?

Finish the picture.

3
2
1

Write the number. _____

Your Turn

Make up your own story about Polly Possum. See if a friend can find out how many floors are in the building.

Name _____

Cheese and Tea

Mimi Mouse is going to Marta Mole's house for cheese and tea. Marta gives these directions, "Start at your house. Go forward 6 blocks on Cheddar Street to Jack Street. Turn right and go forward 5 blocks to Swiss Street. Turn left and go 3 blocks to 10 Swiss Street." Can you show the path to Marta's house?

Finish the map.
Show Mimi's path.

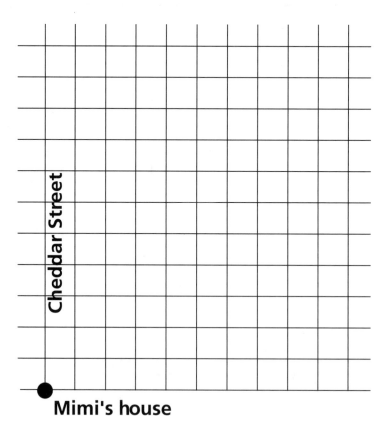

Cheddar Street

Mimi's house

Doing More

Write directions for another way to Marta's house.
Have a friend follow your directions.

Teaching Plan for Story Problem 13

Dinos Out for a Ride

A yellow dino, a red dino, and two blue dinos are out for a ride in a car. The dino who is driving is not yellow or blue. A blue dino is sitting behind a yellow dino. What color is each dino in the car?

Give children some dinos and a copy of page 19.

Find Out and Talk About It

- Where are the dinos? *Out for a ride in a car*
- What color are the dinos in the car? *A yellow, a red, and two blue*
- What do we know about the dino who is driving? *This dino is not yellow or blue*
- What do we know about the blue dinos? *One blue dino is sitting behind a yellow dino*
- What do we have to find out to solve the problem? *What color each dino is in the car*

Use Strategies

- We can use a special kind of thinking, called "logical thinking." We can use this kind of thinking and the clues to help us solve this problem.
- Would it help to move dinos around to find out what color each dino is in the car? *Yes* Using things, or objects, to act out the problem is a good way to solve some problems.

Solve It

- What color dinos shall we use? *1 yellow, 1 red, and 2 blue*
- Let's start with the dino driving the car. If this dino is not yellow or blue, what color is it? *Red*
- Where shall we put the yellow dino? *If a blue dino is behind the yellow dino, then the yellow dino must be in the front seat beside the red dino.*
- Now where do we put one blue dino? *Behind the yellow dino*
- Where does the other blue dino sit? *In the back seat behind the red dino*

Check It

Read the problem again and have the children check to see if the positions of the dinos match the conditions in the problem.

Give children a copy of page 20.

Marta Mole's Summer Reading

Marta is choosing one of these books to take out of the library.

Here are some clues to tell you which book Marta took home:

• Marta hates to cook.
• It is about things that have engines and motors.
• It is about things that don't fly.

Which book did Marta take home?

Find Out and Talk About It

• What was Marta Mole doing? *Choosing a book from the library*
• What were the books about? (Let the children describe the books from looking at the book covers.)
• What clues do you have about the book that Marta took home? *Marta hates cooking; the book is about things with engines and motors, and it's about things that don't fly.*
• What do we have to find out to solve this problem? *Which book Marta took home*

Use Strategies

• We can use a special kind of thinking, called "logical thinking." We can use this kind of thinking and the clues to help us solve this problem.

Solve It

• Let's use the first clue as we look at the pictures of the book covers. Marta hates to cook. Does this clue tell us about any of the books that it could not be? *Yes, the book about cooking desserts.* We can cross out this book.
• What is the second clue? *The book is about things that have motors and engines.* How many books will fit this clue? *2* Can it be the whales or dogs? *No, because whales and dogs don't have a motor or engine.* We can cross out the books about whales and dogs.
• What's the third clue? *The book is about things that don't fly.* Look at the books that aren't crossed out. Is there one about something that doesn't fly? *Yes* Then we can cross out the book about planes.
• Which book fits all the clues? *The book about trains*

Check It

Read the problem again and have the children check to see if the book matches all the clues.

Name _____

13 Dinos Out for a Ride

A yellow dino, a red dino, and two blue dinos are out for a ride in a car. The dino who is driving is not yellow or blue. A blue dino is sitting behind a yellow dino. What color is each dino in the car?

Color the dinos in the car.

Your Turn

Put the dinos in the car in a different way. Make up a story problem about the dinos. See if a friend can solve your problem.

Marta Mole's Summer Reading

Marta is choosing one of these books to take out of the library.

Here are some clues to tell you which book Marta took home:

- Marta hates to cook.
- It is about things that have engines and motors.
- It is about things that don't fly.

Which book did Marta take home?

Color the book Marta took home.

Your Turn

Write clues about the book Marta likes best. Let a friend use your clues to find the book Marta likes best.

Name _____

At Bear's Play

A green dino, a red dino, a blue dino, and a yellow dino are at Bear's play. There are two rows of dinos, with two dinos in each row. There are no green dinos in the second row. A yellow dino is sitting behind a red dino. Where could the dinos be sitting?

Color the dinos in the rows.

Your Turn

Put the dinos in the rows in a different way. Make up your own story problem about the dinos. See if a friend can solve your problem.

Get Your Hands on Problem Solving, Grade 2 © Ideal

Name _____

Dana Dino's Backyard Friend

Dana looks for his favorite backyard friend.

Dana gives these clues about his favorite backyard friend:

- It flies.
- It doesn't have feathers.
- It stings.

Which backyard friend is Dana's favorite?

Color the friend that Dana likes best.

Your Turn

Write clues about the friend Dana likes best. Ask a partner to use your clues to find the friend Dana likes best.

Name _____

Use Logical Thinking
Act out with

17

Dinos on the Bus

Two yellow dinos, two red dinos, and two blue dinos are out for a ride in Flora Frog's double-decker bus. A red dino is sitting above a red dino. A yellow dino is between a blue dino and a red dino. A blue dino is below a yellow dino and in front of a red dino. Where are the dinos sitting on the bus?

Color the dinos in the bus.

Your Turn

Put the dinos in the bus in a different way. Make up a story about the dinos. See if a friend can solve your problem.

23

Name _____

Leaping Frog Summer Camp

Flora Frog is choosing her favorite sport at summer camp.

Here are some clues about the sport she likes best:

- She uses a ball.
- She doesn't use a racquet.
- She doesn't use a bat.

Which sport is Flora's favorite?

Color the picture that shows Flora's favorite sport.

Your Turn

Write clues about the sport Freddy Frog likes best. Let a friend use your clues to find the sport Freddy likes best.

Teaching Plan for Story Problem 19

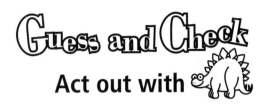

Bear's Barbecue
There are 4 red dinos, 3 green dinos, and 5 yellow dinos eating at Bear's Barbecue. There are three picnic tables in a row. Each table has one color of dinos at it. There are 9 dinos altogether at tables 1 and 2. There are 8 dinos altogether at tables 2 and 3. What color are the dinos at each table?

*Give children some dinos
and a copy of page 27.*

Find Out and Talk About It

- Where are the dinos? *At Bear's Barbecue* What are the dinos doing? *Sitting at picnic tables* How many tables are there? *3* What else do we know about the picnic tables? *They are in a row; and there is one color of dinos at each table.*
- How many red dinos are there? *4* How many green? *3* How many yellow? *5*
- How many dinos in all are at tables 1 and 2? *9*
- How many dinos in all are at tables 2 and 3? *8*
- What do we have to find out to solve the problem? *What color the dinos are at each table*

Use Strategies

- To help us solve this problem, we can make guesses and check to see if our guesses are right.
- Would it help to make groups of dinos and move them around to find out what color dino is at each table? *Yes* Using things, or objects, to act out the problem is a good way to solve some problems.

Solve It

- Let's make a guess. Where should we put the 4 red dinos? *At the first table* Where shall we put the 3 green dinos? *At the second table* (Children might begin with other guesses.) How many dinos are at tables 1 and 2 now? *7*
- That's too low. Let's make another guess. What dinos shall we put at table 1? *3 green* What dinos shall we put at table 2? *5 yellow* How many dinos are at tables 1 and 2 now? *8*
- Let's try another guess. What color shall we put at table 1? *4 red* Table 2? *5 yellow* How many dinos do we have altogether at tables 1 and 2 now? *9*
- Now how many will go at table 3? *3 green*
- How many dinos are there altogether at tables 2 and 3? *8*

Check It

Read the problem again and have the children check to see if the numbers of dinos at the tables match the conditions in the problem.

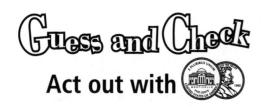

Act out with

> **②⓪ Roland's Bad Day**
> Roland Rabbit hops off to McRabbits for a lettuce and carrot sub. When he gets there, he finds his pocket is empty. He hops back to look for his coins. When he left home, he had 35 cents. He had two kinds of coins: pennies and nickels. He had two times as many pennies as nickels. What coins should Roland look for?

Give children some play coins and a copy of page 28.

Find Out and Talk About It

- Where is Roland going? *To get a sub at McRabbits*
- What happens to him? *He gets there and his pocket is empty*
- How much money did Roland have when he left home? *35 cents*
- How many different kind of coins did he have? *2* What are the two different kinds? *Pennies and nickels*
- What do we know about the number of pennies and nickels? *There were two times as many pennies as nickels.*
- What do we have to find out to solve the problem? *What coins Roland is looking for*

Use Strategies

- To help us solve this problem, we can make guesses and check to see if our guesses are right.
- Would it help to make groups of pennies and nickels and move them around to find out what coins Roland had? *Yes* Using things, or objects, to act out the problem is a good way to solve some problems.

Solve It

- Let's make a guess. How many nickels do you think he had? *2* (Children might begin with other guesses.)
- If he has 2 nickels, then how many pennies does he have? *4*
- How much does he have altogether? *14 cents*
- That's not enough money. Let's make another guess. How many nickels does he have? *4* Then how many pennies does he have? *8* How much does he have altogether? *28 cents*
- Let's try another guess. How many nickels? *5* How many pennies? *10* What are his coins worth altogether? *35 cents*

Check It

Read the problem again and have the children check to see if the numbers of coins match the conditions in the problem.

Name _____

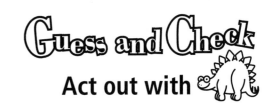

19 Bear's Barbecue

There are 4 red dinos, 3 green dinos, and 5 yellow dinos eating at Bear's Barbecue. There are three picnic tables in a row. Each table has one color of dinos at it. There are 9 dinos altogether at tables 1 and 2. There are 8 dinos altogether at tables 2 and 3. What color are the dinos at each table?

Table 1 _____   Table 2 _____

Table 3 _____

Your Turn

Make up a new problem about the dinos at Bear's Barbecue. Write clues for your problem. Can a friend solve your problem?

Name _____

 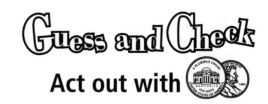

Roland's Bad Day

Roland Rabbit hops off to McRabbits for a lettuce and carrot sub. When he gets there, he finds his pocket is empty. He hops back to look for his coins. When he left home, he had 35 cents. He had two kinds of coins: pennies and nickels. He had two times as many pennies as nickels. What coins should Roland look for?

Pennies _____   Nickels _____

Doing More

What if Roland had:

• Three kinds of coins: pennies, nickels, dimes
• The same number of dimes as nickels
• Three more pennies than dimes

What coins would Roland need to look for?

Name _____

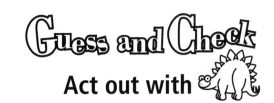
21 The Jungle Surprise Ride

There are 7 yellow dinos, 6 blue dinos, and 5 red dinos waiting for the Jungle Surprise Ride to begin. Three boats are lined up. There is one color of dinos in each boat. There are 11 dinos altogether in boats 1 and 2. There are 13 dinos altogether in boats 1 and 3. What color are the dinos in each boat?

Boat 1 _____   Boat 2 _____

Boat 3 _____

Your Turn

Make up a new problem about the dinos at the Jungle Surprise ride. Write clues for your problem. Can a friend solve your problem?

Name _____

The Forest Fair

Flora Frog and Polly Possum are putting their coins together at the Forest Fair. They both want a ride on the Spinning Cars. They have three kinds of coins: pennies, nickels, and dimes. Together the coins are worth 63 cents. They have the same number of dimes as pennies. They have three more nickels than dimes. What coins do they have?

Pennies _____   Nickels _____   Dimes _____

Doing More

What if Flora and Polly had:

• Three kinds of coins: pennies, nickels, dimes
• One more nickel than dimes
• Ten more pennies than dimes

What coins would Flora and Polly have?

Get Your Hands on Problem Solving, Grade 2 © Ideal

Name _____

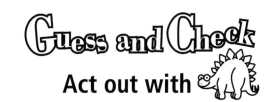

Circus Clown Cars

The dino clowns are ready! There are 9 yellow dinos, 8 green dinos, 3 red dinos, and 4 blue dinos. There are four clown cars lined up and each car has one color of dinos in it. There are 11 dinos in cars 1 and 2. There are 7 dinos in cars 2 and 3. What color are the dinos in each clown car?

Car 1 _____ Car 2 _____

Car 3 _____ Car 4 _____

Your Turn

Make up a new problem about the clown dinos. Write clues for your problem. Can a friend solve your problem?

Name _____

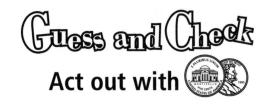
24 Mole's Munchies

Dolly Dog and Polly Possum are in line at Mole's Munchies. Together they have 85 cents for a snack. They have three kinds of coins: nickels, dimes, and quarters. They have the same number of nickels and dimes. They have fewer quarters than dimes. What coins do they have?

Nickels _____   Dimes _____   Quarters _____

Doing More

What if Dolly and Polly had:
- Three kinds of coins: pennies, nickels, dimes
- Two times as many nickels as dimes
- One more penny than dimes

What coins would Dolly and Polly have?

Teaching Plan for Story Problem 25

Act out with

㉕ Matt's Old Stuff
Matt Mouse was selling some of his old stuff at a garage sale. Mimi Mouse loves to buy old stuff. She bought some things and gave Matt 3 pennies and 3 other coins. She paid less than 33 cents, but more than a quarter. How much did Mimi spend?

Give children some play coins and a copy of page 35.

Find Out and Talk About It

- What was Matt doing? *Selling old stuff at a garage sale*
- What did Mimi do? *She bought some of Matt's things*
- What coins did she give Matt? *3 pennies and 3 other coins*
- What do we know about the amount Mimi paid? *She paid less than 33 cents, but more than a quarter.* How many cents is that? *25*
- What do we have to find out to solve this problem? *How much Mimi spent*

Use Strategies

- To help us solve this problem, we can make a table to keep track of the amounts Mimi could have spent.
- Would it help to use play coins to check the clues? *Yes* Acting out problems with objects can help us solve some problems.

Solve It

- The problem tells us that Mimi spent more than 25 cents. Let's start the table with that amount. What is the highest number we need in our table? *33, because Mimi spent less than 33 cents*
- Fill in the amounts between 25 and 33. Can we cross out 25? *Yes, because Mimi paid more than a quarter.* Can we cross out 33? *Yes, because Mimi paid less than 33 cents.*
- What else do we know about the amount? *Mimi gave Matt 3 pennies and 3 other coins.* Let's use coins to find an amount that we can make with 3 pennies and 3 other coins. Can we make 26 cents? *No* Cross it out. 27 cents? *No* Cross it out. 28 cents? *Yes* 29 cents? *No* Cross it out. 30? *No* 31? *No* 32? *No* What number is not crossed out? *28*

Check It

Read the problem again and have the children check to see if their solution matches the conditions of the problem.

 Freddy Frog's Ferry Boat
Freddy Frog is taking dinos across the river on his ferry boat. Freddy takes 3 red dinos and 4 green dinos on each trip. When 15 red dinos have crossed the river, how many green dinos have crossed?

*Give children some dinosaurs
and a copy of page 36.*

Find Out and Talk About It

• What is Freddy Frog doing? *Taking dinos across the river on his ferry boat*
• What do we know about the dinos Freddy takes across on each trip? *He takes 3 red dinos and 4 green dinos on each trip.*
• What do we have to find out to solve this problem? *How many green dinos are across the river when 15 red dinos have crossed*

Use Strategies

• To help us solve this problem, we can make a table to keep track of the dinos who cross the river.
• Would it help to use dinosaurs to show what is happening in the story problem? *Yes* Acting out story problems with objects can help us solve some problems.

Solve It

• Let's act out the story problem with our dinosaurs. What colors of dinosaurs shall we use? *Red and green*
• If Freddy Frog makes one trip across the river, how many red dinos will be across the river? *3* Let's write 3 in the table. How many green dinos? *4* Let's write 4 in the table.
• If Freddy makes two trips, how many red dinos will be across the river? *6* How many green dinos? *8*
• If Freddy makes three trips, how many red dinos will be across the river? *9* How many green dinos? *12*
• If Freddy makes four trips, how many red dinos will be across the river? *12* How many green dinos? *16*
• If Freddy makes five trips, how many red dinos will be across the river? *15* How many green dinos? *20*

Check It

Read the problem again and have the children check to see if the numbers in their table match the conditions of the problem.

Name _____

Matt's Old Stuff

Matt Mouse was selling some of his old stuff at a garage sale. Mimi Mouse loves to buy old stuff. She bought some things and gave Matt 3 pennies and 3 other coins. She paid less than 33 cents, but more than a quarter. How much did Mimi spend?

Finish the table.

25	33

Write the amount. _____

Your Turn

Write your own story problem about Mimi buying old stuff. Let a friend solve your problem.

Name _____

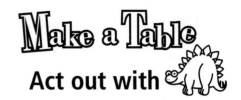

Make a Table

Act out with

26

Freddy Frog's Ferry Boat

Freddy Frog is taking dinos across the river on his ferry boat. Freddy takes 3 red dinos and 4 green dinos on each trip. When 15 red dinos have crossed the river, how many green dinos have crossed?

Fill in the table.

Number of Trips	Total Number of Dinos Across the River	
	Red	Green
1	3	
2	6	

Write the number. _____

Doing More

Look for a pattern in the numbers in your table. Can you tell how many green dinos will be across the river when there are 21 red dinos?

Name _____

Make a Table

Act out with 🪙

27 Lunch at Carla Cat's Café

Bernie Bear bought honey pie for lunch in Carla Cat's Café. He paid less than 30 cents, but more than 20 cents. He gave Carla 2 dimes and 4 other coins. How much did Bernie pay?

Make a table.

_____

_____

Write the amount. _____

Doing More

Bernie was still hungry, so he bought some catfish soup. He gave Carla 4 nickels and 2 other coins. He paid more than 22 cents, but less than 32 cents. How much did Bernie pay?

Name _____

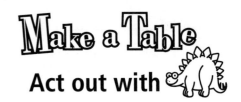

A Scary Walk

The dinos are at summer camp. It is a dark night, and they are going on a scary walk! The dinos are walking in groups. Each group has 3 yellow dinos and 5 blue dinos in it. If there are 25 blue dinos on the walk, how many yellow dinos are there?

Fill in the table.

Number of Groups	Total Number of Dinos on the Scary Walk	
	Yellow	Blue

Write the number. _____

Your Turn

Write your own story problem about groups of dinos on a scary walk. Let a friend try to solve your problem.

Name _____

29

Possum Playland

Polly Possum and her friends are at Possum Playland.
Polly bought a ticket to go on the Rocking Rocket.
She paid with 1 quarter and 2 other coins. The ride
cost more than 35 cents, but less than 45 cents.
How much did Polly pay?

Make a table.

_____

_____

Write the amount. _____

Your Turn

Write your own story problem about Polly and her friends
buying tickets. Let a friend try to solve your problem.

Name _____

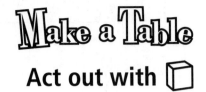
30

Bessie's Beads

Bessie Bear is getting ready for a big sale in her bead shop. She is putting beads in bags. She puts 5 orange beads and 8 brown beads in each bag. When there are 30 orange beads in bags, how many brown beads are in the bags?

Fill in the table.

Number of Bags	Total Number of Beads in the Bags	
	Yellow	Blue

Write the number. _____

Doing More

Look for a pattern in the numbers in your table. When there are 64 brown beads in bags, how many orange beads will there be in the bags?

Act out with

31

Pig and His Camera
Pig took pictures of 3 blue dinos and 3 yellow dinos. There were 2 dinos in each picture, and every picture was different. One picture had 2 blue dinos in it. What colors were the dinos in the other pictures?

Give children some dinosaurs and a copy of page 43.

Find Out and Talk About It

- What did Pig do? *He took pictures of dinos*
- How many blue dinos were there? *3* How many yellow dinos? *3*
- How many dinos were in each picture? *2* What else do we know about the dinos in the pictures? *Every picture was different.*
- What colors were the dinos in one picture? *2 blue*
- Did Pig take another picture of two blue dinos together? *No, because every picture was different.*
- What do we have to find out to solve this problem? *What colors the dinos were in the other pictures*

Use Strategies

- To help us solve this problem, we can make an organized list, a step-by-step list. Making this kind of list helps us keep track of the dinos in the pictures. It also makes it easy for us to see that we have found **all** of the pairs of dinos in pictures.
- Would it help to move dinos around to find all the different pairs? *Yes* Acting out problems with objects is a good way to solve some problems.

Solve It

- What colors of dinosaurs shall we use? *Blue and yellow*
- How many blue dinos shall we take? *3* How many yellow dinos? *3*
- What colors are the dinos in one picture? *Blue, blue* Let's put those 2 blue dinos together. We can write *blue, blue* in the list.
- What colors could the dinos be in another picture? *Blue and yellow* Let's put a blue dino and a yellow dino together, then write *blue, yellow* in the list.
- What colors are the dinos we have left? *2 yellow* Let's put them together and write *yellow, yellow* in the list.

Check It

Read the problem again and have the children check to see if the colors in their list match the conditions of the problem.

Raccoon Race

Bonnie Bug is buying a ticket for the big Raccoon Race. The ticket costs 15 cents. Bonnie has pennies, nickels, and dimes. What are all the groups of coins Bonnie could use to pay for the ticket?

Give children some play coins and a copy of page 44.

Find Out and Talk About It

- What is Bonnie Bug doing? *Buying a ticket for the Raccoon Race*
- How much does a ticket cost? *15 cents*
- What do we know the coins Bonnie has? *She has dimes, nickels, and pennies.*
- What do we have to find out to solve this problem? *All the groups of coins Bonnie could use to pay for the ticket*

Use Strategies

- To help us solve this problem, we can make an organized list. Making this kind of list helps us keep track of the groups of coins Bonnie could use to pay 15 cents for the ticket. The list makes it easy for us to see that we have found **all** of the groups.
- Would it help to use play coins to find all the groups? *Yes* Acting out story problems with objects is a good way to solve some problems.

Solve It

- What coins should we use? *Pennies, nickels, and dimes*
- What is one group of coins that would equal 15 cents? *1 dime and 1 nickel* (Encourage children to find their own organized way of finding all of the groups. Some may begin with the dime and nickel, others may prefer to begin with 15 pennies.)
- What is another group of coins that would equal 15 cents? (Continue in the same way until the children have found all possible ways of combining coins to make 15 cents.)

Check It

Read the problem again and have the children check to see if every possible group of coins is in their list, and if they match the conditions of the problem.

Name _____

 31

Pig and His Camera

Pig took pictures of 3 blue dinos and 3 yellow dinos. There were 2 dinos in each picture, and every picture was different. One picture had 2 blue dinos in it. What colors were the dinos in the other pictures?

Finish the list.

Picture	Colors of Dinos
1	blue, blue
2	
3	

Doing More

Now 3 green dinos and 3 red dinos ask Pig to take their pictures. What colors will the two dinos be in each picture?

Name _____

32

Raccoon Race

Bonnie Bug is buying a ticket for the big Raccoon Race. The ticket costs 15 cents. Bonnie has pennies, nickels, and dimes. What are all the groups of coins Bonnie could use to pay for the ticket?

Finish the list.

15 Cents

Dimes	Nickels	Pennies
1	1	0
1	0	5

Doing More

If Bonnie gives the ticket seller 11 coins to pay for the ticket, what coins are they?

Get Your Hands on Problem Solving, Grade 2 © Ideal

Name _____

Make an Organized List
Act out with 🦕

33 **Playing Tic-Tac-Toe**

Four red dinos, 4 yellow dinos, and 4 blue dinos are playing tic-tac-toe. There are 2 players at each tic-tac-toe board, and every pair is different. What colors are the dinos at each tic-tac-toe board?

Finish the list.

Tic-Tac-Toe Board	Colors of Dinos
1	
2	
3	
4	
5	
6	

Your Turn

Write your own story problem about dinos playing a game. Let a friend find all the different pairs of players.

Make an Organized List

Act out with

(34) **Marta's Money**

Marta Mole is saving money for a train trip. Her mother has some dimes, nickels, and pennies in her pocket. She gives 20 cents to Marta for taking care of her baby brother. What are all the groups of coins Marta could have?

Finish the list.

20 Cents

Dimes	Nickels	Pennies
2	0	0

Doing More

If Marta's mother gave her 8 coins worth 20 cents, what coins were they?

Get Your Hands on Problem Solving, Grade 2 © Ideal

Act out with

35

Catch the Ball!

Three green dinos, 3 blue dinos, 3 yellow dinos, and 3 red dinos are throwing and catching balls. They are practicing in pairs. If every pair is different, what colors are the dinos in each pair?

Finish the list.

Pair	Colors of Dinos
1	
2	
3	
4	
5	
6	

Doing More

Now the dinos are practicing in groups of 3. Every group is different. What colors are the dinos in each group?

Name _____

(36)

Dusty Dog

It's a sunny day at the beach. Dusty Dog is hot and thirsty. He has some dimes, nickels, and pennies in his backpack. He takes some out and buys a giant sno-bone for 21 cents. What are all the groups of coins Dusty could use?

Finish the list.

21 Cents

Dimes	Nickels	Pennies

Doing More

If Dusty used 8 coins to pay for the sno-bone, what coins were they?

Coins and Nuts

Oh dear! Sally Squirrel dropped her coins when she buried a nut. She had three kinds of coins: nickels, dimes, and quarters. Sally had coins worth 65 cents. She had one more dime than nickels, and one more nickel than quarters. What coins should she look for?

Nickels _____   Dimes _____   Quarters _____

What did you use to solve the problem?

Act Out With	Look for a Pattern	Guess and Check
Act Out With	Use Logical Thinking	Make a Table
Act Out With	Make a Picture	Make an Organized List

Name _____

Roland's Robot Factory

Roland Rabbit is busy making robots in his factory. He is making 24 robots for Turtle's Toy Shop. The robots are lined up on a table in this order: yellow, brown, yellow, orange, yellow, brown, yellow, orange. If Roland keeps using the same pattern, how many robots will there be of each color?

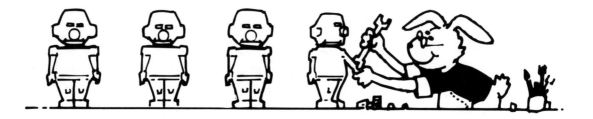

Write the colors and numbers.

_____   _____   _____

What did you use to solve the problem?

Act Out With 🦕	Look for a Pattern	Guess and Check
Act Out With 🪙	Use Logical Thinking	Make a Table
Act Out With ▢	Make a Picture	Make an Organized List

Name _____

Flora Frog's Coins

Flora Frog bought a backpack in Sam Snake's Shop.
She paid more than 50 cents, but less than 60 cents.
She gave Sam 2 quarters and 3 other coins. How
much did Flora spend?

Write the amount. _____

What did you use to solve the problem?

Act Out With 🦕	Look for a Pattern	Guess and Check
Act Out With 🪙	Use Logical Thinking	Make a Table
Act Out With ▢	Make a Picture	Make an Organized List

40

How Do You Like to Travel?

Carla Cat is voting for her favorite way to travel.

Here are some clues to tell you which is Carla's favorite:

• This way is not on streets.
• This way is not in the air.
• Carla does not like to travel on water.

Which way does Carla like to travel?

Color the picture that shows the way Carla likes best.

What did you use to solve the problem?

Act Out With	Look for a Pattern	Guess and Check
Act Out With 🪙	Use Logical Thinking	Make a Table
Act Out With ⬜	Make a Picture	Make an Organized List

Name _____

41 The Crow Condos

Benny the Mailbird is delivering mail to the birdhouses in the Crow Condos. The birdhouses are on a pole. Benny starts at the lowest one. From there he flies up 5 birdhouses. Then he flies down 3 birdhouses. Finally he flies up 5 birdhouses to the top one. How many birdhouses are in Crow Condos?

Write the number. _____

What did you use to solve the problem?

Act Out With	Look for a Pattern	Guess and Check
Act Out With	Use Logical Thinking	Make a Table
Act Out With	Make a Picture	Make an Organized List

Get Your Hands on Problem Solving, Grade 2 © Ideal

Name _____

Mice on Mars

When Matt Mouse leaves the movie, he finds he has lost his coins. Matt had four different kinds of coins: pennies, nickels, dimes, and quarters. The coins were worth 98 cents. Matt had the same number of quarters and dimes. He had two times as many pennies as nickels. What coins should he look for?

Pennies _____   Nickels _____   Dimes _____

Quarters _____

What did you use to solve the problem?

Act Out With 🦕	Look for a Pattern	Guess and Check
Act Out With 🪙	Use Logical Thinking	Make a Table
Act Out With ⬜	Make a Picture	Make an Organized List

Name _____

Peter Packrat's Socks

Peter Packrat has 4 green socks, 4 purple socks, and 4 orange socks. He likes to wear a different pair of socks every day. Sometimes Peter wears two socks that are the same color. Sometimes he wears two socks that are not the same color! What are the colors of the socks in each pair?

Show the colors in each pair.

What did you use to solve the problem?

Act Out With 🦕	Look for a Pattern	Guess and Check
Act Out With 🪙	Use Logical Thinking	Make a Table
Act Out With ⬜	Make a Picture	Make an Organized List

Name _____

Sticker Club

Diana Dino started a sticker club. There were 3 dinos at the first meeting, and 5 dinos at the second meeting. There were 7 dinos at the third meeting, and 9 dinos at the fourth meeting. If the pattern continued, how many dinos were at the sixth meeting of Diana's sticker club?

Write the number. _____

What did you use to solve the problem?

Act Out With	Look for a Pattern	Guess and Check
Act Out With	Use Logical Thinking	Make a Table
Act Out With	Make a Picture	Make an Organized List

Get Your Hands on Problem Solving, Grade 2 © Ideal

Name _____

The Dino Show

The dinos are on stage. There are 2 blue dinos, 2 green dinos, 1 red dino, and 1 yellow dino. The dinos are in two lines. There are 3 dinos in each line. A red dino is dancing between 2 blue dinos. A yellow dino is dancing in front of a blue dino. Where are the dancing dinos in the lines?

Color the dinos.

What did you use to solve the problem?

Act Out With	Look for a Pattern	Guess and Check
Act Out With	Use Logical Thinking	Make a Table
Act Out With	Make a Picture	Make an Organized List

Name _____

Wheelbarrow Race

Four green dinos, 4 blue dinos, and 4 yellow dinos are having a wheelbarrow race. They are racing in groups of 3. Every group is different. What colors are the dinos in each group?

Show the colors in each group.

What did you use to solve the problem?

Act Out With	Look for a Pattern	Guess and Check
Act Out With	Use Logical Thinking	Make a Table
Act Out With	Make a Picture	Make an Organized List

Name _____

Beaver Park Pool

Berta Beaver invited Tammy Toad to Beaver Park Pool. Berta gave her these directions: "Start at your house. Go 2 blocks up Pond Street to Garden Street. Turn right on Garden Street and go forward 4 blocks to Water Street. Turn left on Water Street and go forward 5 blocks to Main Street. Turn right on Main Street and go forward 3 blocks. You will be at Beaver Park Pool." Can you show Tammy's path to the pool?

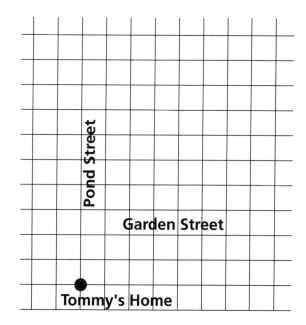

What did you use to solve the problem?

Act Out With 🦕	Look for a Pattern	Guess and Check
Act Out With 🪙	Use Logical Thinking	Make a Table
Act Out With ⬜	Make a Picture	Make an Organized List

Name _____

Toy Dinos

Trudy Turtle is unpacking boxes of toy dinos for her toy store. Each box has 4 red dinos and 8 green dinos in it. As Trudy takes the dinos out of the boxes, she puts them on a shelf. When there are 28 red dinos on the shelf, how many green dinos will be on the shelf with them?

Write the number. _____

What did you use to solve the problem?

Act Out With 	Look for a Pattern	Guess and Check
Act Out With	Use Logical Thinking	Make a Table
Act Out With	Make a Picture	Make an Organized List

Name _____

Jumping Toads

Tammy Toad and her friends had jumping contests today. There were 4 toads in the first round. There were 7 toads in the second round. More toads kept coming to join the fun. There were 10 toads in the third round, and 13 in the fourth round. If the pattern continued, how many toads were there in the sixth round?

Write the number. _____

What did you use to solve the problem?

Act Out With 🦕	Look for a Pattern	Guess and Check
Act Out With 🪙	Use Logical Thinking	Make a Table
Act Out With ⬜	Make a Picture	Make an Organized List

Name _____

Lily Lizard's T-Shirts

Lily Lizard sells T-shirts of all sizes for 25 cents.
Albert Alligator came into the shop and bought
a T-shirt. He took some pennies, nickels, and dimes
out of his backpack to pay for the T-shirt. What are
all the groups of coins Albert could use?

Show all the groups.

What did you use to solve the problem?

Act Out With	Look for a Pattern	Guess and Check
Act Out With	Use Logical Thinking	Make a Table
Act Out With	Make a Picture	Make an Organized List

51 Purple Submarine

Bonnie Bug took some beetle scouts on dives in her purple submarine. On every dive, she took 5 blue beetles and 7 yellow beetles down to see the octopus. After quite a few trips, Bonnie counted 35 yellow beetles who had been on dives. Then she started to count the blue beetles. How many blue beetles had been on dives?

Write the number. _____

What did you use to solve the problem?

Act Out With	Look for a Pattern	Guess and Check
Act Out With	Use Logical Thinking	Make a Table
Act Out With	Make a Picture	Make an Organized List

52

The Flying Dinos

The dinos are ready to take off! There are 10 red dinos, 12 green dinos, 9 yellow dinos, and 8 blue dinos at the airport. There are four planes lined up. Each plane has one color of dinos in it. There are 18 dinos altogether in planes 1 and 2. There are 19 dinos altogether in planes 2 and 3. What color are the dinos in each plane?

Plane 1 _____   Plane 2 _____

Plane 3 _____   Plane 4 _____

What did you use to solve the problem?

Act Out With	Look for a Pattern	Guess and Check
Act Out With	Use Logical Thinking	Make a Table
Act Out With	Make a Picture	Make an Organized List